LO

ANIMAL MONSTERS

The Truth About Scary Creatures

Laurence Pringle

MARSHALL CAVENDISH   NEW YORK

Library of Congress Cataloging-in-Publication Data
Pringle, Laurence P.
Animal monsters : the truth about scary creatures / by Laurence Pringle
p.   cm.   Includes bibliographical references and index.
Summary: Describes a variety of scary animals, including the alligator, black widow spider, and mountain lion.
ISBN 0-7614-5003-3
1. Dangerous animals—Juvenile literature. 2. Monsters—Juvenile literature. [1. Dangerous animals.] I. Title
QL100.P75 1998   591—dc20   96-27604   CIP   AC

Cover photo: *The National Audubon Society Collection/Photo Researchers, Inc.*: Ken M. Highfill
Cover inserts: *The National Audubon Society Collection/Photo Researchers, Inc.*: Tim Davis, left; Scott
Camazine, center; G.C. Kelley, right

The photographs in this book are used by permission and through the courtesy of: *The Image Bank*:
Flip Chalfant, 8; Mercury Archives, 45; J. Carmichael, Jr., 49. *The National Audubon Society Collection/Photo
Researchers, Inc.*: J.H. Robinson, 10; Tom McHugh, 13, 39, 54; Renee Lynn, 14; Richard Ellis, 16;
Tim Davis, 19, 31, 60; Scott Camazine, 22; Jerry L. Ferrara, 25; London Daily Mail, 26; A. Gragera,
Latin Stock/Science Photo Library, 28; Gregory Ochocki, 34; Tom McHugh, Steinhart Aquarium, 37;
Stephen Dalton, 42; Helen Williams, 52. *Animals Animals*: Michael Fogden, 57.

CONTENTS

MONSTERS OF THE MIND, OR REAL MONSTERS?

Just a thousand years ago, it seemed that monsters were everywhere. In Europe, fierce dragons killed livestock and people. Men called giants, twenty feet tall, stalked the land. And huge sea serpents rose from the ocean depths to attack sailing ships.

We are lucky to live in a time when these monsters no longer exist. But wait a minute—what happened to them? Did they die out? No, actually they never existed—except in the imaginations of the people who lived in those times.

The Middle Ages, which ended about five hundred years ago, were times of great ignorance. People had odd beliefs and superstitions about the causes of disease, droughts, earthquakes, and other happenings in nature. Often they blamed powerful monsters. Many people also believed in other fantastic creatures: unicorns, tiny elves, mermaids.

Clearly, we should never underestimate the power of the human imagination! It not only "creates" monsters and mermaids, but helps spark the creativity of explorers, inventors, artists—everyone. And even today, when we know so much more about nature and life on earth, people still use their imaginations to create monsters. Why? Well, almost everyone enjoys a good scare now and then. That's why spooky mystery stories, horror films, and roller coaster rides are so popular. Most people enjoy feeling a tingle of fear, especially when they know they are really safe—while watching television, for example.

In 1993, John Hedricks, chairman of the Discovery channel, explained why an entire week featured documentary films about sharks: "What we have learned," he said, "is if an animal can eat you, ratings go through the roof."

People also want to be mystified, to let their imaginations run wild. Perhaps the human desire to wonder is stronger than the desire to understand. So people continue to "create" animal monsters. Oh, they don't believe in dragons and giants any more, but some think the Loch Ness monster is real, and people often believe that real animals are much more dangerous than they actually are.

Alas, the truth is usually less scary and exciting than people want to hear. Some animals with such words as "killer," "devil," or "monster" as part of their names rarely harm people. However, there are animals that can hurt and even kill humans. Some are just as dangerous as people believe, some are not. You can learn the truth about these creatures in this book. You can also learn about a few "monsters" that live only in the wildest habitat on Earth: the human imagination.

ALLIGATOR

Ten-year-old Bradley Weidenhamer stepped from a canoe into the Florida's Loxahatchee River and began trying to haul the canoe over a log. Suddenly a huge alligator lunged from the water, seized the boy and pulled him under.

Bradley's father grabbed his son's foot and pulled back. People in nearby boats tried to hit the alligator with oars. The 'gator let the boy go, but Bradley later died of head and chest wounds inflicted by the alligator. When it was caught and killed, it measured more than eleven feet long and weighed 400 pounds.

This tragedy occurred in 1993. The alligators' normal range extends throughout the southern United States from North Carolina to Texas. While they rarely attack humans, every few years an American alligator does kill someone in the United States. Children are especially vulnerable, while adults are usually able to fight their way free. Victims usually die from drowning rather than from wounds because alligators tend to pull their prey underwater, hold it in a mighty grip until it stops struggling, then store it for later feeding.

Alligators sometimes kill dogs that are swimming or playing at the water's edge. Dogs are close in size to fish, muskrats, raccoons, opossums, and other animals that are the natural prey of a large alligator. Alligators are shy, wary reptiles that usually avoid people. However, in Florida alone there are more than a million alligators. They live in freshwater habitats—lakes, rivers, canals, marshes—that are visited by millions of people. Many golf course ponds harbor one or more alligators.

Encounters between 'gators and humans are inevitable, yet only a few people are hurt each year. Often people invite trouble by feeding alligators, perhaps to show off a big reptile to visiting relatives or friends. Though state laws forbid it, they toss marshmallows or other treats to a 'gator. The alligator begins to lose its fear of humans. Then one day it may mistake someone's white sneaker for a big marshmallow.

With all its strength, stealth, and eighty spiked teeth, the American alligator could easily kill dozens of people every year. It doesn't, and it will be even less of a threat if people respect its wildness.

BLACK WIDOW SPIDER

A widow is a woman whose husband has died and who has not remarried. Certain kinds of small spiders are called widows because they, too, commonly lose their mates. They *make themselves* widows because they sometimes kill their male partners after mating. They kill them for food—a husband is an after-mating snack!

In North America, the most widespread widow spider is called the black widow. It lives in every state on the continent except Alaska but is most common in the warmer, more southern states. A black widow spider is only about a half inch long. The male has a tiny abdomen and is harmless. The female has a round, glossy black abdomen, usually marked underneath with bright red. She also has a deadly bite.

The venom of a black widow female is among the most powerful of all animal venoms. It is fifteen times stronger than that of a prairie rattlesnake. Fortunately, a spider bite delivers only a tiny dose of this venom. That is still strong enough to make a person very sick, and sometimes to cause death.

A black widow's bite does not cause pain and may not be noticed. Its effects begin to appear an hour or so later. The venom is a neurotoxin—a chemical brew that affects a person's nervous system. One chemical in particular attacks nerves where they attach to muscles. It can cause agonizing muscle pain and spasms, breathing difficulty, nausea, and an irregular heart beat. These symptoms may last for three to four days. In very rare cases the toxin causes the lungs to stop working and the victim dies.

GREATLY ENLARGED

Black widows bite only in self-defense, or to kill insects for food. They build small webs in dry, shady places, usually near the ground, in woodpiles, stone walls, and in sheds, garages, and barns. Watch out for them in such places, and never touch any small spider with a glossy black abdomen.

Female spiders of all kinds, large or small, have a venomous bite, but their fangs are usually too small to break through human skin or their venom is too weak to affect people. In addition to widow spiders, one other kind of North American spider can harm people. The half-inch-long brown recluse spider, most common in the South, has a toxin that kills muscle tissue and causes wounds that may not heal for months.

Remedies called antivenins are available for the bites of brown recluse and widow spiders. So the bite of a black widow is rarely fatal, but the spider continues to have a scary name and deadly reputation.

CROCODILE

Crocodiles seem to smile. Their grins, however, are just the result of the shape of their closed jaws, with some big sharp teeth still showing. Their snouts are more pointed than those of alligators. About four hundred and fifty American crocodiles survive in southern Florida. Like alligators, they avoid people. Elsewhere in the world, however, several kinds of crocodiles are fast, agile predators that sometimes stalk and attack human beings.

A large crocodile, seeing a person by the shore of a river, can submerge and swim underwater directly to its target. It gets within a few feet without making a ripple. That's too close for comfort, since a crocodile can outrun a human in a short race on land.

In Africa, the Nile crocodile is the largest of three crocodile species. It grows as long as twenty feet, and is powerful enough to overcome water buffalo and zebras. Each year Nile crocodiles kill several people in Africa.

Even larger crocodiles live in parts of Australia, New Guinea, and Indonesia. These saltwater crocodiles may grow longer than twenty feet. "Salties," as they are sometimes called, usually live in the salty water along coasts, in mangrove swamps and estuaries, but visit fresh-water rivers too. Their last great stronghold is northern Australia.

Like the American alligator, the giant saltwater crocodile of this area was once in danger of extinction. Given protection, its numbers grew. And as the population expanded, crocodiles spread out into settled areas where people use the rivers and other waters for recreation. Big

crocodiles sometimes ambush swimmers and even attack small boats.

In Darwin, the largest city in northern Australia, patrols kill the largest crocodiles that venture near beaches. However, most crocodiles are still protected. Many tourists visit northern Australia to see crocodiles and would be disappointed if these scary reptiles were gone. So both residents and visitors are given safety tips to help them avoid unpleasant meetings with the giant saltwater crocodile.

GILA MONSTER

Suppose that you were asked to make a drawing of a creature called the gila (pronounced *heela*) monster. Say the name again: GILA MONSTER. From the name alone you would probably draw something big and nasty. The actual "monster" is a two-foot-long, slow-moving lizard that lives in the southwestern United States and Mexico.

Both the gila monster and its larger cousin, the beaded lizard of Mexico, have a poisonous bite. When one of these lizards grabs a bird or small mammal, it holds on tightly. Venom flows from glands located along the edges of its lower jaw. Without breaking its grip the gila monster chews, wounding the animal's skin and allowing the venom to enter its victim's blood stream.

The gila monster bites prey animals to get food but bites people only to defend itself. In humans the venom causes weakness, dizziness, and sharp pain. In a few rare cases it has caused death, but only a powerful imagination can make this shy lizard, which does its best to avoid people, into a genuine monster.

GREAT WHITE SHARK

The words "bull shark" sounds scary. Say "tiger shark" and a shiver may run down your spine. But no shark name can match the terror induced by these words: "great white shark." They conjure up the terrible vision of a triangular gray fin slicing through the water toward you, of dying in those powerful jaws. Ever since Peter Benchley's 1974 novel *Jaws* and the 1975 film adapted from it, millions of people have felt a little bit nervous about venturing into the ocean for a swim.

The great white is a superpredator: a fast swimmer with many sharp teeth and powerful senses that detect vibrations in the water as well as blood and other chemical clues produced by prey animals. However, the real shark—not the one in *Jaws* or in human imagination—is not nearly as dangerous as people believe. It bites people mostly by accident, then spits them out. It is not a man-eater.

More than three hundred and fifty species of sharks live on earth. Bull sharks and tiger sharks harm more people than the great white. Bull sharks live in the tropics, and swim up freshwater rivers, including the Amazon and even the Lower Mississippi. Tiger sharks, named for the dark stripes on their backs, also live mostly in tropical waters. The great white lives in cooler, temperate waters. In the summertime it ranges as far north as Alaska and Nova Scotia.

The great white shark is not white; it has a white belly with a deep blue or gray-green top. However, it can be "great," measuring more than twenty feet and weighing a ton and a half. Large adults feed on large prey: seals, sea lions, sea turtles, fish, squid, and dolphins.

People are about the same size as the animals that great whites usually eat. To a shark, a surfer or diver in a dark-colored wet suit may look like a seal. From below, a person in a kayak or a surfer paddling on a small surfboard may also look like a swimming seal.

Scientists believe that great white shark attacks on people are almost all cases of mistaken identity. After its first bite, the shark usually releases the person. One possible explanation is that people don't taste good! When great white sharks are offered bait, they bite but release lean meat. They prefer blubbery chunks of whale, seal, or sea lion.

Most people who are attacked survive. Worldwide there are only about fifty to seventy-five shark attacks that result in five to ten deaths each year. Considering the millions of people who play in the water for billions of hours each year, sharks are far from the monsters we imagine them to be. In 1991, South Africa passed a law that protects great white sharks. Along the California coast, the emphasis is on safety tips for people, not killing sharks, which are overfished all over the world.

GRIZZLY BEAR

When Blackfoot Indians roamed what is now western Canada, they met bears of two kinds. One was the black bear, which can weigh six hundred pounds and stand six feet tall. Black bears are impressive animals, but the Indians recognized the enormous size, strength, and speed of a second species. The Blackfeet called it the *real bear*. It was the grizzly.

A full-grown grizzly weighs over eight hundred pounds and stands seven feet tall. Its usual color is dark brown, though some individuals are more gray or yellow. Often the hair on a bear's upper body looks frosted. It is tipped with white—grizzled—and so the bear is called the grizzly. Its scientific name is *Ursus arctos horribilis*. The grizzly is called *horribilis* because it can be aggressive. It sometimes kills and eats people.

Many thousands of grizzly bears live in western Canada and Alaska. Less than a thousand survive in the western United States, mostly in Yellowstone National Park and Glacier National Park. Millions of people visit these parks each year. Most visitors are never in danger from grizzlies because they do not venture into the wild lands the bears prefer. The people at greatest risk are those who hike, fish, or camp deep in the wilderness.

All bears are omnivores; they eat all sorts of plant and animal food. Though grizzlies are powerful enough to kill elk, moose, and other large mammals, most of their daily diet consists of grasses, roots, berries, nuts, insects, and mice. They do not normally hunt humans,

but may attack when they are hungry and are attracted to the food people have with them. Getting close to a mother grizzly's cubs is especially dangerous. In 1987 a mother grizzly killed a photographer in Glacier National Park after he had stalked the bear and her three cubs.

Film in his camera showed that he had approached to within sixty yards of the bears. When the mother bear charged, he tried to climb a tree to safety. Unlike black bears, grizzlies are poor climbers because their claws are nearly straight, not curved. Nevertheless, broken branches and claw marks reached twenty feet up the tree—evidence that the photographer was dragged down.

People who explore wilderness areas where grizzlies live are advised to deliberately make noise to avoid surprising a bear. Campers are also especially cautious in the spring when bears emerge from hibernation and are particularly hungry. The actual number of people killed by grizzlies is small—fewer than twenty since 1900 in the lower forty-eight states. Black bears have killed more, but this is because they are much more common and widespread than grizzlies. They have more contact with humans. Black bears usually flee from people. In its wild Western habitat, the grizzly is still the *real bear*.

KILLER BEE

In July 1993, Lino Lopez, a rancher in southern Texas, tried to burn a nest of bees in the wall of a house. He was stung hundreds of times and was pronounced dead when brought to a hospital. Actually he drowned, as bee venom caused his lungs to fill with fluid. Lino Lopez was the first person in the United States to die from the stings of killer bees.

Mention the name "killer bee" to people and many will imagine a big, aggressive insect that travels in large swarms that swoop down to attack people. Mention the name to scientists who study insects (entomologists) and they might say, "That name—killer bee—is misleading and an exaggeration. I call them African or Africanized bees."

This honeybee with a terrible reputation came originally from central and southern Africa. In the 1950s, queen honeybees from Africa were brought to Brazil for research. Some were let go accidentally, some on purpose. The African bees thrived and spread. They mated with other, more docile varieties of honeybees, but the new generations seemed to be as feisty as their African parents. As African bees spread in South America and advanced into Central America, they were named "killer bees" by journalists. The bees crossed into Texas from Mexico in 1990. At that point, thirty-three years after their release in Brazil, African bees had killed between seven hundred and a thousand people, and many more dogs, pigs, cows, and other animals.

African bees do not look like monsters. They are slightly smaller than the varieties of honeybees that live in the United States and

Canada. Also, they are not aggressive. They do not go looking for trouble. Rather, they are ready when "trouble" comes to them.

A person or animal that approaches a colony of African bees is often seen as a threat to the colony—to its store of honey, and to its young bees. When a worker bee releases an alarm scent, hundreds or even thousands of other workers rush to defend their colony. Each worker bee carries a venomous stinger at the tip of its abdomen. In defend-

ing their colony, African bees may stay alarmed, ready to sting, for hours.

Most people who accidentally spark this fierce defense are able to run away and suffer only a few stings. Nearly all of the people (and animals) who have died could not flee. Most victims are older men, disabled people, or young children. Several hundred beestings can be life-threatening to anyone but are especially dangerous for children. A dose of bee venom is more concentrated in a child's body than in a larger adult body. (The same is true of poison from a widow spider, snake, scorpion, or other venomous animal.)

African honeybees are tropical insects, and will not be able to survive winter temperatures in most of the United States and Canada. They have spread to southern New Mexico, Arizona, and California, and are expected to live in Florida and in the warmer regions of several southern states. As the bees have advanced into new territory, state and city governments have launched educational programs to help avoid trouble with these ornery insects.

Even before killer bees reached the United States, about forty people died each year from the stings of honeybees, yellow jackets, and other stinging insects. (In a sense, this means that honeybees are much more dangerous than grizzly bears or alligators.) Ordinarily the sting of a bee, wasp, or hornet is not life-threatening. However, about four people out of every thousand are allergic to bee venom. A single sting can be fatal. People who are highly allergic to bee venom can carry special medicine that stops the allergic reaction.

KOMODO DRAGON

In the early 1970s, Dr. Walter Auffenberg spent thirteen months on small Indonesian islands that are the home of the world's largest lizard, the Komodo dragon. He discovered that the lizards were intelligent, rather tame, and curious about humans. Some were noticeably more aggressive toward people than others. One large male on Komodo Island had a special interest in people: it had killed and eaten three of them.

Dr. Auffenberg named this lizard 34W. One day he found the footprints of 34W along a beach, showing that it had been following his children. His family grew more cautious. "When I left I recommended to the Indonesian government that they kill 34W, because he was a proven menace," he said. "But the officials refused. Some time later, a tourist disappeared while walking through 34W's range, and although a bloody shirt and a camera case were found, the tourist never reappeared."

A few thousand Komodo dragons live on Komodo, Flores, Padar, and a few other small islands in Indonesia. They live nowhere else on earth. Newly hatched from eggs, these monitor lizards are only about a foot long and weigh three ounces. At first they live in trees, catching insects and small lizards. As full-grown adults, ten feet long and often weighing more than two-hundred pounds, they stalk or ambush large prey: deer, wild pigs, goats, and fellow dragons, as well as an occasional human.

For a short distance, Komodo dragons can run eleven miles an hour—fast enough to catch a person. Their teeth have sawtooth edges, enabling them to tear off chunks of flesh. They can gulp down half a pig in one bite—legs, feet, and all. Meat caught on their jagged tooth edges rots there, and is home for some nasty bacteria. People have died from infections that resulted from a Komodo dragon bite.

The dragons are scavengers as well as predators. They can detect the scent of rotting flesh from far away. Sometimes their hunt for food leads them to cemeteries where they dig up corpses.

On Komodo Island, park officials arrange a dragon-feeding frenzy for tourists, who watch several big ones feasting on a dead goat. Visitors are also given a safety tip: don't go hiking alone.

LOCH NESS MONSTER

A deep valley bisects Scotland and in it lies Loch Ness, twenty-three miles long and more than a mile wide. The lake is nearly a thousand feet deep at one point. Its animal life is well known and includes trout, salmon, pike, eels, and river otters. People lived by and fished in Loch Ness for centuries without catching or seeing anything out of the ordinary, except for one report of a "huge fish" in 1868.

Reports of the Loch Ness monster began in 1934 when a London surgeon produced a photograph he said he had taken at the loch. It showed a long-necked creature with a small head rearing up from the loch's surface. This famous image, since  shown countless times in publications and on television, brought worldwide attention to Loch Ness. Tourists and journalists began to visit the loch in hopes of getting a look at the monster.

Through the years many hundreds of people claimed to have seen the Loch Ness monster. According to a few who swear they saw it on land in their auto headlights, the creature is about twenty-five feet long. Out in the loch, a beast up to fifty feet long, with a small head and a long, tapering neck is reported. It comes to the surface for only a few minutes, then slips back into the dark, peat-stained waters.

Though big, the creature is no monster; it has never laid a claw or tooth on anyone, so it is affectionately called Nessie. Many people, including a few scientists, believe that a population of Nessies live in the loch. Perhaps they are descendants of zeuglodons—slender whales thought to have been extinct for at least 20 million years. The most likely ancestors, it is claimed, are plesiosaurs—long-necked fish-eating reptiles thought to have been extinct for about 65 million years.

Although millions of people enjoy believing that the Loch Ness monster exists, scientists who know the loch well, and who weigh evidence carefully, say there is no Nessie. The notion that Loch Ness is the earth's only refuge for zeuglodons or plesiosaurs from millions of years ago is especially far-fetched. Just a few thousand years ago Loch Ness did not exist; its valley was filled with a mile-high glacier.

The best evidence for the existence of any creature is physical evidence—the animal itself, dead or alive, or at least its skeleton. Otters, fish, and every other kind of creature that lives in Loch Ness are known from physical evidence. Somehow, a population of Nessies has never left a carcass or skeleton on the loch shore. Signs of feeding and footprints are also physical evidence. The most distinct set of monster footprints ever found by Loch Ness were identified as those of a young hippopotamus. Is Nessie a hippo? No, the tracks were made on the shore by pressing a hippo's foot, which had been made into an umbrella holder, into the mud.

The hippo tracks are just one example of several tricks, or hoaxes, that were aimed to fool people into believing that the Loch Ness monster exists. Through the years several photographs have been shown to be fakes, and in 1994 the famous original 1934 photograph of Nessie was also revealed to be a hoax. A man who helped create the "monster" told how he shaped its head and neck out of wood and attached it to a toy submarine. After the "monster" was photographed

in the water, a respected London doctor was asked to pretend he took the photos. He went along with the joke, which became one of the most successful hoaxes of the twentieth century.

Eager for some solid evidence of the loch monster, expeditions have produced fuzzy underwater photographs that could be part of a large beast—or of a submerged tree. A sonar device detected a large bulky object at a depth of 230 feet. It was identified as an airplane that had ditched in the loch in 1940.

In 1994, a spokesman for the Loch Ness Project, which continues to search for Nessie, said, "Eyewitness accounts still suggest that there is something powerful in the loch."

Lacking physical evidence or trustworthy photographs, eyewitness accounts are the only remaining evidence that one or more monsters lurk in the loch. More than three thousand people claim to have seen Nessie. Scientists, however, are skeptical about these sightings. The words "I saw it with my own eyes" are powerful, but in courts of law, eyewitness testimony is not considered very reliable.

If ten people witness an auto accident, investigators often get ten different accounts of what occurred. Research has shown that what people report seeing can be influenced by their expectations and desires. One group of people, deprived of food, "saw" food items in a series of blurred images that were projected on a screen. The hungrier they became, the more food they "saw."

Since many people visit Loch Ness hoping to see Nessie, it is understandable that some of them see something like a monster on the lake's surface. What do they see? According to scientists who are familiar with Loch Ness, they see mostly otters, "mirages" caused by light being refracted over the water surface, or stern waves of boats passing through the loch. Waves left by a boat travel long distances and may be seen several minutes after the boat is out of sight. They often appear as a moving line of dark humps. To most people these waves look like, well, waves. To others they look like the undulating back of a lake monster.

Once Nessie became world famous, people reported seeing monsters living in some other large bodies of water. "Chessie" has been sighted in Chesapeake Bay, "Champ" in New York's Lake Champlain, "Manipogo" in Canada's Lake Manitoba. Sightings of harmless monsters are good for the tourist business. People see things out there on the water's surface, but not one bit of physical evidence has been found that lake monsters exist.

MOUNTAIN LION

On an April morning in 1994, a forty-year-old woman named Barbara Schoener ran alone on an isolated trail in a recreation area northeast of Sacramento, California. On the hillside above the trail a mountain lion waited for a deer or another wild mammal that is its normal prey. The mountain lion killed Barbara Schoener. It ate part of her body, then covered it with sticks and leaves, hiding it for safekeeping as cats do.

A human, even a large man, is easy prey for a mountain lion. A big lion weighing less than two hundred pounds can kill a moose or an elk that weighs eight hundred. A mountain lion is not a pack animal like the wolf. It hunts alone, but its strength, speed, stealth, claws, and teeth make it the king of North American predators.

The mountain lion once lived all across the North American continent, and was given several different names: cougar, puma, panther, painter. It was nearly wiped out by ranchers and other settlers, and now lives in the wilder parts of several western states, southwestern Canada, and Mexico. (East of the Mississippi, about two hundred panthers survive in southern Florida.) With hunting now regulated or barred entirely in some states, its numbers have increased. The mountain lion usually avoids people. However, as homes are built near wilderness lands and more and more people use these lands for recreation, the numbers of puma-people encounters also grow.

Mountain lions are masters at sneaking up on prey. Their human victims have included several children. When a California cougar was seen hidden by a schoolyard watching children play, wildlife officials

decided that this aggressive individual should be shot. The mountain lions of Vancouver Island, British Columbia, seem especially aggressive toward humans. Of all the mountain lion attacks on humans in the United States and Canada between 1890 and 1990, more than a third occurred on Vancouver Island and more than half in British Columbia.

There have been only fifty-three attacks on people in a hundred years. Nine were fatal. So the mountain lion is hardly an animal monster. However, encounters and attacks are increasing and wildlife biologists offer safety tips to people who live in or visit cougar country.

A mountain lion is more likely to attack a child or small person than a big one, so parents are urged to keep children close to them while hiking. Also, never run from a mountain lion. Running may stimulate the cat to chase and attack. Stand tall, make lots of noise, and, if necessary, fight back with hands, a stick, or whatever weapon might be at hand. This behavior has saved people from attack, or enabled them to fend off an aggressive mountain lion.

OCTOPUS

Imagine this scene: a diver swims by the entrance to an underwater cave. Suddenly an octopus tentacle encircles the diver's body. Another tentacle, then another, clutch the diver, who is pulled closer, closer to the monster's snapping beak.

The octopus has been called the "devil fish." It has been described in novels, and shown in movies and television films, as a huge, powerful beast that attacks divers. Although fiction writers and filmmakers still use the octopus as a villain, their stories are pure make-believe. The octopus doesn't grow as big as people imagine. Most species are only about two feet long. One specimen of the largest species—called the giant octopus—weighed nearly six hundred pounds and its tentacles spanned thirty-one feet. However, this species normally weights about fifty pounds with a tentacle span of eight to ten feet.

In 1995, scientists were able to use modern techniques to identify the preserved remains of sea creatures that had been called octopus monsters. One was the decayed remains of a 150-foot-long animal that had washed ashore on a Florida beach in 1896. Many people believed it was the carcass of a monstrous octopus. In 1988 another, smaller mass of flesh was found on a Bermuda beach. It was called the Bermuda Blob, and some people thought it, too, was the remains of a huge octopus. Tissue samples from both "monsters" were saved. Recent chemical studies have shown that neither creature was an octopus. The Florida carcass was the remains of a warm-blooded animal, probably a humpback whale. The Bermuda Blob was probably a shark.

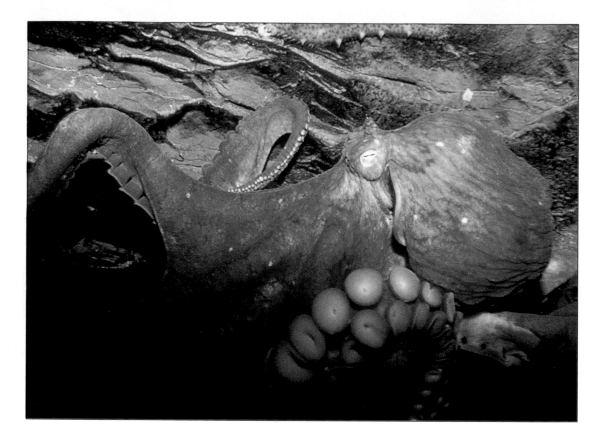

So there are no huge octopuses. More important, with the exception of one Australian species that has a powerful venom, the octopus is simply not a threat to people. It is a shy creature that tries to hide from divers and never attacks, even if provoked. In fact, the octopus is greatly admired by marine biologists—the people who know it best.

The octopus is a mollusk, related to slugs and snails. Most mollusks aren't noted for their intelligence, but the octopus has a large, well-developed brain. It can solve puzzles, for example, unscrewing the lid of a jar to reach food. It is a fast learner, at least as smart as a cat, and is clearly the most intelligent of all the animals without backbones.

With its beak the octopus cracks open the shells of clams, crabs, lobsters, and other prey, then eats the contents. Often it first stuns its prey by releasing a poison into the water. Just one species—the blue-ring octopus of Australia—is dangerous to humans. Its toxin affects the human nervous system. One peck from the beak of this small octopus can cause death in a few hours. People who have foolishly picked up this eight-inch long octopus have died, because the octopus defends itself from what it sees as an animal monster: a human.

PIRANHA

"Tooth fish" is the meaning of "piranha," the name given to about thirty species of fish that live in the freshwater rivers and lakes of South and Central America. Their teeth are triangular and very sharp. For many centuries Indians removed the jaws of dead piranhas and used them as cutting tools. In fact, along parts of the Amazon River the word "piranha" also means "scissors."

Piranha teeth also serve as useful tools for filmmakers, especially those who want to dispose of a villain in a jungle adventure film. The "bad guy" seems to be getting away. All he has to do is wade or swim across a river. Partway across, piranhas strike. As they attack, the water seems to boil and soon runs red with the victim's blood. In a short time all that remains is a skeleton.

There is a bit of truth in such stories, but most kinds of piranhas pose no threat to people. Some species eat mostly seeds and fruits that fall into the water. Others nip off scales and parts of fins from other fish. A few big species, up to two feet long, are capable of killing a human. Powerful jaw muscles combined with razor sharp teeth enable these piranhas to quickly chop off flesh. According to one report that seems reliable, several hundred piranhas reduced the carcass of a hundred-pound capybara to its skeleton in less than a minute.

Although hungry piranhas could attack and eat a person, this seems to be a rare event. The discovery of a human skeleton in the water only demonstrates that piranha are both predators and scavengers. They commonly clean the flesh from the bodies of people, livestock, and wild animals that drowned or died of other causes. Throughout the range of the piranha, children and adults swim in the rivers and lakes where this fish lives. Divers have swum among piranha, filming them, and have not been harmed.

Certain conditions may cause piranhas to attack a person. In the dry season, rivers shrink in size and many piranhas may be crowded together—and very hungry. Muddy waters, with poor visibility, increase the risk that piranhas will accidentally bite a person. People in South and Central America have learned not to swim near an animal carcass, or near a slaughterhouse, where the wastes would attract piranhas.

Even though there are few proven cases of piranha attacks on people, it is foolish to attract the attention of the "tooth fish."

RATTLESNAKE

One of the scariest sounds in nature is not a mighty roar but a slight, buzzing, whirring noise. It sounds like someone shaking a baby rattle, or a tiny castanet. It is the sound of a rattlesnake shaking its tail tip where a string of hollow, interlocking segments form a rattle.

A rattlesnake avoids people and other large creatures that might harm it. Its rattle is a warning: "I am here; watch your step!" Nevertheless, each year several thousand people are bitten and about ten die from the venomous bite of a rattlesnake. Many victims are men who are asking for trouble, showing off by handling a snake or teasing one they find by the side of a road.

Thirty species of rattlesnake live in North America. They are all pit vipers, a group of venomous snakes named for special heat-sensing organs located in little pits between their eyes and nostrils. In North America the pit vipers also include copperheads and moccasins, which do not have rattles.

Of the North American rattlesnakes, the prairie rattlesnake has the widest range, but other kinds of rattlers—western, timber, and sidewinder—account for more bites because they have more encounters with humans. Most deaths are caused by bites of eastern diamondback and western diamondback rattlesnakes, which have a more powerful venom. (Other kinds of venomous snakes, including the eastern coral snake that lives in several southern states, have stronger venom than any rattlesnake.)

Normally, a rattlesnake lies in wait for a mouse, ground squirrel, or

other small prey. Day or night, it relies mostly on its heat-sensing powers to detect warmth given off by an animal. When coiled up the snake can strike outward about half the length of its body. Within milliseconds it injects venom through hollow fangs into the victim. Then it lets its prey go.

The animal runs on. Sometimes it escapes, for some rattlesnake strikes fail to inject any venom. More often the prey does not get very far. The venom causes tissues and blood vessels to break down. Blood floods the animal's body and its organs stop working. It dies quickly. The venom actually begins to digest the body before the snake finds it.

After waiting patiently, the rattlesnake follows the trail of its prey, not by sight, not by heat-sensing organs, but by scent. Its forked tongue flicks in and out rapidly, gathering scent information from the air and inserting it into sensory organs located in the roof of its mouth. Once the prey is found the snake swallows it whole.

A rattlesnake can adjust the amount of venom released—a little for a mouse, a lot for a person who is about to step on the snake. Painful swelling soon follows but antivenin medicine halts the effects of the venom. Even without antivenin, or when antivenin treatment is delayed, most people survive the bite of a rattlesnake, though some effects of the venom may linger for months.

Some states now protect their rattlesnake populations. They want these fascinating reptiles to survive in wild parklands where they lived long before humans came to North America. Rattlesnakes do their best to avoid people, and if human visitors use caution and common sense they will probably never hear that slight but scary sound of a rattlesnake's warning.

SCORPION

The death toll caused by such huge animal "monsters" as great white sharks and saltwater crocodiles is tiny when compared with deaths caused by two-to-four-inch-long scorpions. Although hospitals and clinics have antivenin medicine to treat victims of scorpion stings, each year scorpions kill several thousand people. Most deaths occur in Mexico, South America, India, and North Africa where scorpions are most plentiful. Many victims are young children in tropical and subtropical lands, who often play and explore barefoot and without caution. Also, venom from a scorpion sting is more deadly in the small body of a child than in an adult.

A scorpion's stinger is located at the tip of its tail. Its venom is a mixture of several chemicals that affect animal nervous systems. Venom from one African species killed an adult man in just seven hours.

Although the scorpion's bad reputation is well-deserved, there is no reason to fear all scorpions. About fifteen hundred kinds of scorpions have been identified so far, and biologists expect to discover several hundred more. Of all known species, just twenty-five, or two percent, have venom strong enough to kill people. This means that ninety-eight percent of all scorpion species are not the monsters that people imagine them to be. In many cases, a scorpion sting is no more painful than a beesting.

Normally, scorpion venom is used to paralyze prey. Most scorpions feed on insects, spiders, centipedes, and even other scorpions.

Gripping a paralyzed animal in its pincers, a scorpion pours chemicals called enzymes into its body. The enzymes digest the animal into a liquid that the scorpion sucks into its stomach.

Scorpions avoid humans, but without meaning to, people offer them many good hiding places in and near their homes. After a night of hunting, a scorpion welcomes the shelter of a shoe or some clothing. Scorpions live in all sorts of habitats, not just in deserts but also along beaches, high on mountains, and in caves, grasslands, and rain

forests. About thirty species live in the United States, and one can even be found in southwestern Canada.

Just one species found in the United States has a venom that is deadly to humans. Called the sculptured *Centruroides*, it lives mostly in northern Mexico but can also be found in parts of the Southwest. It has one characteristic in common with all deadly scorpions: slender, fragile-looking pincers. These pedipalps, as they are called, are not very good at grabbing and crushing prey. So the scorpion relies on another weapon, its venom. The presence of thin little pincers is a warning that a scorpion has a powerful and perhaps deadly venom.

One of the scariest-looking of all scorpions is the emperor scorpion of Africa. Its shiny black body measures up to eight inches long. But look at its pincers. They are large and powerful. The emperor scorpion relies on its massive pincers to catch and hold prey, and rarely uses its mild venom. This remarkable species, which dwells in colonies, is living proof that sinister looks can be deceiving.

SEA SERPENT

According to tales told by sailors or written in ships' logs by sea captains, there were once ocean monsters. The sight of them frightened ships' crews. In some reports, the monster plucked men from boats and carried them down, down into the ocean depths.

The kraken of Norway was one such fabled monster. It lived in sea caves along the Scandinavian coast, and slithered onto land to gobble up livestock or snatched men from ships at sea. Its scaly body reportedly measured two hundred feet long. The kraken also had a two-foot-long mane.

A mane of hair on a reptilelike creature is remarkable. The body of a kraken would be a fascinating object for biologists to study. However, no such physical evidence has ever been found. And, remember, most reports of sea serpents were written several centuries ago, when people also believed in dragons, and sailors "saw" mermaids.

Still, stories of sea monsters persist, and people who want to believe in their existence argue that large creatures can live undetected in the vast, unexplored world of the oceans. As evidence, they point to the megamouth shark. It was unknown until 1976, when a fifteen-foot-long specimen was caught near Hawaii. Since then only a few other individuals have been captured.

If a large shark was undiscovered until 1976, why can't there still be sea serpents and other monsters lurking in the ocean depths? One reason, say marine biologists, is that the oceans are now being fished and explored as never before. The oceans' "mysterious depths" are not

nearly as mysterious as they were as recently as the 1970s. Also, though it is fun to believe in sea serpents, "sightings" are more likely the result of people misidentifying normal phenomena in nature.

Whether on a large lake or on the ocean, an unusual wave pattern can look like the moving coils of a sea serpent's back. A traveling group of dolphins, rising to breathe, can also look like the undulating back of a marine monster. And there are large sea creatures—whales, squid, and oarfish—that can stimulate the human imagination to "see" a sea serpent.

Among the great whales is the sperm whale; up to sixty feet long, it dives a half mile deep hunting for giant squid. Giant squid, sometimes called kraken after the mythical monster of Norway, can also grow to sixty feet in length, and have the biggest of all animal eyes—the size of dinner plates. Some people believe that monstrous squid must exist. The evidence they cite is the round scars left on the heads of sperm whales that have battled with giant squid. The scars are left by the suckers of a squid's arms. Some sucker scars are double the size of the suckers found on any squid ever found. Does this mean that monster squid, more than a hundred feet long, live in the sea?

Although the scars are a kind of physical evidence, whale experts say that the scars on a whale's body expand in size as the whale grows. So especially big scars do not prove that true giant squid exist.

Everyone knows a little about whales and squids, but few people have heard of the oarfish—another large creature that might be mistaken for a sea serpent. It, too, usually lives in the ocean depths. Up to forty feet long, it wriggles through the water like a giant eel. With tall red spines rising from its head, the oarfish is a scary sight. However, it is harmless to humans; like the megamouth shark, the oarfish is toothless and filters tiny plants and animals from the water.

Fascinating real animals do live in the oceans, but there is no reliable evidence that sea serpents or other unknown monsters do.

TARANTULA

All but one of the spiders in the 1990 film called *Arachnophobia* (which means "fear of spiders") were good-sized but harmless delena spiders from New Zealand. More than three hundred delenas appeared in the film. One was shown creeping into a bedroom slipper. Another crawled out from under a toilet seat.

One other spider appeared in the film: the main villain of *Arachnophobia*. It had to be big and scary looking. It had to be a tarantula.

The spiders we call tarantulas are more correctly called hairy mygalomorphs. They are also called bird spiders because some are capable of catching small birds, as well as lizards and snakes, for their food. Tarantulas include the biggest spider on earth—a species from the Amazon region of South America with a body about three-and-a-half-inches long and a leg span of ten inches. Its fangs are almost an inch long.

Tarantulas frequently appear in films, especially when the story calls for the hero or heroine to be threatened by a big hairy spider. In real life, however, there is no reason to fear any of the thirty species of tarantulas that live in the southwestern United States. Some South American species have a more powerful venom. However, tarantulas are shy and avoid people whenever possible. They bite in self-defense. Though the venomous bite of some species can be painful, tarantulas do not kill people.

Tarantulas do, however, have a second defense: their hairs. The hairs are easily knocked loose. Each one has a sharp tip and is covered

with tiny barbs. A spider researcher, Samuel Marshall, described how a tarantula released some of her hairs in self-defense when he dug into her burrow: "She responded by brushing a rear leg rapidly downward across the rear of her abdomen, releasing a small cloud of shed hairs. Suddenly, my hands and throat were burning and itching furiously, a sensation that persisted for several days."

Tarantula hairs are not poisonous, but their sharp barbs irritate skin. When a pet tarantula is handled roughly, it eventually sheds all of its defensive hairs and develops a bald patch on its abdomen. When gently handled, however, most kinds of tarantulas do not shed hairs or bite. The big shaggy spiders are hardly the villains they are often thought to be.

TASMANIAN DEVIL

In the darkness of night, sometimes even a little sound—a twig snapping, a low growl—can be frightening. One of the scariest of all night sounds, however, is the scream of the Tasmanian devil. It is fierce, loud, blood-curdling, and remarkable because it comes from an animal the size of a big house cat.

The Tasmanian devil once lived in Australia but now survives only on the island of Tasmania, which lies south of the Australian continent. Like kangaroos and many other mammals of the area, it is a marsupial. Right after being born, little devils crawl into their mother's pouch, where they spend about fifteen weeks nursing and growing. After emerging from the pouch the young spend several more months with Mom, first in a nest, then tagging along when she goes hunting. From then on they lead solitary lives.

Early settlers of Tasmania told stories of devils chasing and killing livestock, and even attacking people. But a fully grown Tasmanian devil stands about a foot tall and weighs no more than twenty pounds. How did such a small mammal get such a nasty reputation (which led to its scary name)?

The Tasmanian devil is a predator armed with forty-two teeth and powerful jaw muscles. It can easily kill geese, chickens, and other small farm animals, but normally raids the nests of birds, catches lizards, and eats insects, seeds, and fruits. Like the Komodo dragon, the Tasmanian devil can detect the scent of rotting flesh from far away, then hurries to feast on an animal carcass.

By their nature, two devils at a carcass aren't inclined to share. They emit terrible screams and often fight. Big devils commonly kill and eat smaller ones. In fact, the Tasmanian devil is one of the most aggressive of all mammals. Besides its scream, which can be heard for miles, it has a vocabulary of growls, huffs, lip licks, and tooth clicks that all say, "Watch out! I'm tough!" It sends the same message by stomping its feet and baring its teeth.

You may have seen a cartoon Tasmanian devil whirling around like a tornado. No animal can do this, but this cartoon is based on the real devil's arsenal of threats. When one devil is matched against another of equal size, or is trying to defend itself against a dog or other enemy, it immediately begins alternating between two scary positions. The devil flashes a view of its side, making itself look as big as possible, then of its front, showing its gaping mouth and teeth. Back and forth, back and forth, the devil whirls, showing two kinds of threats.

Although the Tasmanian devil cannot actually spin like a tornado, and is no threat to humans, it is certainly no angel.

TIGER

The tiger is a special cat. It is the champion of all wild cats, bigger than the lion. It is a solitary, stealthy, powerful predator. And it is one of very few wild animals on earth that may deliberately hunt people.

Tigers once ranged over all of Asia, from snowy Siberia to the jungles of Burma and India, and even into Iran and Turkey. Now three of eight subspecies are extinct and a fourth—the Chinese tiger—is almost gone. Only about two hundred of the largest of all tigers, the Siberian tiger, still survive in the wild. The most abundant subspecies, numbering more than four thousand, is the Bengal tiger of India, Nepal, and Bangladesh.

The Bengal tiger is thriving best in a vast wild area of marshes and mangrove jungle called the Sundarbans, along the border between India and Bangladesh. And in the Sundarbans a few years ago, it was not unusual for tigers to kill fifty people a year.

Most tigers avoid people but some individuals, perhaps five percent of the population, learn that humans are easy prey and good to eat. According to the field director of the Indian Sundarbans Tiger Reserve, this problem begins when a woodcutter, fisherman, or honey gatherer accidentally meets a mother tiger and her cubs. Defending her young, the tigress kills a person for the first time. After that, she may stalk and kill others for food. She may teach her young to hunt people too.

Since only a small part of the tiger population is aggressive toward humans, managers of the tiger reserve have tried to "shock" man-eat-

ing tigers into changing their ways. Lifelike dummies have been set out which deliver a 220-volt jolt when bitten. Some have been attacked, and have caused tigers to flee from people or to avoid the area where they were shocked. This has reduced the death toll by tigers.

People have tried another trick on tigers to reduce the death toll, based on observations of how tigers usually attack humans. Tigers are master stalkers. They usually sneak close to their prey without being detected, then spring from the side or behind. The tiger usually aims for the neck of its prey. Small animals are killed as the tiger breaks their backbone or spinal cord. Larger animals, including buffalo, die for lack of air as the tiger grips their throat.

The cunning tiger waits until a person's back is turned before attacking. In 1989, workers in the Sundarbans mangrove forests were given face masks to wear on the back of their heads. Even though a worker's back might be turned toward a tiger, the mask made it seem that the worker was facing the tiger. The trick worked well as long as people did not become careless with their masks. One woodcutter died when he sat down to eat lunch and took off his mask. Two fishermen were killed by tigers when they left their masks in their boats, then went ashore.

Man-eating tigers get plenty of attention from newspaper and television journalists, but most tigers avoid people—their worst enemy—and simply try to survive in their dwindling wild habitats.

VAMPIRE BAT

In 1565, Girolamo Benzoni, an Italian explorer in Central America, wrote in his journal: "There are many bats which bite people during the night . . . while I was sleeping they bit the toes of my feet so delicately that I felt nothing, and in the morning I found the sheets and mattresses with so much blood that it seemed I had suffered some great injury."

Three kinds of blood-eating bats live in Central and South America. Not much is known about two rather uncommon species, except that one gets its blood meals from birds. Much more is known about the most common species. It has a wide range, takes blood from mammals, and was almost certainly the species that drank blood from Girolamo Benzoni's toes.

Although native Americans had names for these bats, explorers from Europe soon thought of another name—vampire—based on mythical witchlike creatures in Europe that also sought the blood of humans. Being called "vampires" hasn't helped these bats win any wildlife popularity contests! However, the European conquest and settlement of Latin America did eventually affect the night-to-night lives of the bats. For thousands of years the bats had fed mostly on sloths, monkeys, and other native mammals. European settlement brought horses, cows, sheep, and other livestock. Today a colony of vampire bats does not often need to take blood from a sleeping person or a wild mammal because there are whole herds of cattle to feast on.

A vampire bat is a small mammal, weighing less than two ounces.

Its wingspan is only five to six inches. With its wings folded, a vampire bat would fit easily in the palm of your hand. Holding a vampire bat may not appeal to you, but a biologist at Yale University kept one in his laboratory for five years. Gwendolyn, as she was called, enjoyed sitting in his hand and hanging upside down from his shirt pocket.

Like most bats, vampires are intelligent and tame easily. Wild ones have other qualities that people usually admire. Mother vampires take exceptionally good care of their young. Sometimes other members of the bat colony help. If, for example, a nursing mother dies, another female bat adopts the baby, begins to produce milk, and nurses the little bat.

When a young bat is five or six months old, it clings to its mother's fur and is carried out into the night for a lesson on getting its own food of blood. Vampire bats are experts at approaching a cow or other prey animal without being noticed. Whether scrambling over the ground or landing gently from the air, a bat is often able to take a meal of blood without waking its victim.

The bat usually picks a spot where blood vessels are close to the surface. (People are usually bitten on the toes or fingers, and sometimes on the ears and lips.) On livestock a bat usually shears away some hair to expose a small area of skin. Then it cuts out a tiny circle of flesh with its bladelike teeth. Blood seeps out, and a chemical in the bat's saliva prevents the blood from clotting.

A vampire bat cannot suck blood. It laps it up with its tongue, just as a dog laps up water. Usually it takes about an ounce of blood, then flies home.

In many situations, cattle and other livestock are not seriously harmed by vampire bats. However, a horse or cow that is steadily fed upon by several bats may grow weak and lose weight; the cow gives less milk. Also, in certain areas some vampire bats carry a virus that causes the disease rabies. A bite from a rabid bat can kill a cow. In such areas, steps are taken to reduce the numbers of vampire bats. This is a challenging task, because vampire bats often roost in caves or other shelters with highly valued bat species that catch insects or pollinate the flowers of rain forest trees.

Throughout all of South and Central America, few people die from being bitten by rabid vampire bats. In fact, the bats don't often seek fresh human blood. A mythical vampire may "vant your blood," but a real vampire bat is content lapping up its dinner from a cow's neck.

WOLF

In the Middle Ages, many people in Europe believed in dragons and vampires, and also believed that wolves were monsters: savage, cruel, bloodthirsty, evil, worthless. European settlers brought these feelings about the wolf to North America, where they shot, poisoned, and trapped the wolf into near extinction.

Even today, when a child first hears the word "wolf," it is often preceded by "big bad." Still-popular fairy tales teach that wolves eat cute pigs and grandmothers, and try to eat little girls. Many people still believe that wolves are dangerous to humans.

This belief has been thoroughly investigated. Scientists have checked all well-documented reports of wolf "attacks" in North America. No one was seriously injured. No healthy wild wolf has ever killed a person in North America. Elsewhere in the world, most reported wolf attacks have turned out to be tall tales. Some deaths have been caused by rabid wolves, but of course the disease rabies also makes killers of dogs, raccoons, and other mammals.

World famous wolf researcher L. David Mech says, "Over and over again during my career as a wolf biologist I have found that rather than worrying about whether wolves would attack me, I worried how I could get closer to them." While people have no reason to fear wolves, wolves have every reason to fear people, and so they use their intelligence and powerful sense of smell and hearing to avoid humans. Wolves are seldom seen, even in wilderness parks visited by millions of tourists.

In 1995, wolves caught alive in Canada were released in Yellowstone National Park in Wyoming and Montana. For decades, wolf researchers had urged that wolves be brought back to this wild area. The wolves are expected to reduce the size of huge elk herds. Wolves will prey on elk, deer, bison, and other grazing mammals, killing mostly the sick, weak, and old. They will have a positive effect on the overall health of Yellowstone's wildlife.

Although some ranchers in the Yellowstone region opposed the return of the wolf, people all over the United States strongly favored it. Public attitudes towards wolves have changed in the United States and Canada. Although many people still hear those words—"big, bad wolf"—early in their lives, they later see television programs or read books and magazines that tell about *real* wolves. They learn about the close social bonds of wolf packs, their playfulness, their intelligence.

The wolf is the ancestor of the dog, which is called "man's best friend." So, for many people, a creature that was once called an animal monster is now an animal to be admired and respected.

CONCLUSION

The wolf's reputation as a dangerous creature began to change as people discovered what the real animal was like. Perhaps the information in this book about other animals has begun to change your feelings about them, too. Clearly, some creatures with scary names and bad public images are not very dangerous.

The risk can be made even less if people use common sense and follow the safety tips that are in this book and that are also available in parks and other areas where certain wild animals live. In some areas (for example, where people live near growing numbers of alligators or mountain lions) people can feel safe from harm when they learn how to avoid risky encounters with the wildlife.

The animals themselves want to be left alone in their wild habitats. Without them, the habitats would not seem nearly as wild. What a loss it would be, to live in a world where jungles had no tigers, mountains no grizzly bears, and oceans no great white sharks.

Fiction writers and filmmakers will continue to use rather harmless creatures as animal monsters. The human imagination will continue to create monsters. And real animals, not monsters, will continue to make the world an exciting and fascinating place.

INDEX

Page numbers for illustrations are in italics.